BEAUTIFUL
TABLETOP
GARDENS

BEAUTIFUL TABLETOP GARDENS

Janice Eaton Kilby

LARK BOOKS

A Division of Sterling Publishing Co., Inc.
New York

Art Director: Tom Metcalf
Photographer: Steve Mann
Cover Designer: Barbara Zaretsky
Illustrator: Orrin Lundgren & Stacey Gray
Assistant Editor: Rain Newcomb
Production Assistance: Shannon Yokeley, Lorelei Buckley
Editorial Assistance: Delores Gosnell

Special Photography:
Sanoma Syndication
SANOMA Syndication/Alexander van Berge 28, 29, 30
SANOMA Syndication/Dolf Straatemeier 8 (right), 112, 126-127
SANOMA Syndication/Paul Grootes 6, 17, 27, 44, 45, 100, 114, 116

10 9 8 7 6 5 4 3 2 1

First Edition

Published by Lark Books, a division of
Sterling Publishing Co., Inc.
387 Park Avenue South, New York, N.Y. 10016

© 2003, Lark Books

Distributed in Canada by Sterling Publishing,
c/o Canadian Manda Group, One Atlantic Ave., Suite 105
Toronto, Ontario, Canada M6K 3E7

Distributed in the U.K. by Guild of Master Craftsman Publications Ltd., Castle Place, 166 High Street, Lewes, East
Sussex, England
BN7 1XU
Tel: (+ 44) 1273 477374, Fax: (+ 44) 1273 478606, Email: pubs@thegmcgroup.com, Web: www.gmcpublications.com

Distributed in Australia by Capricorn Link (Australia) Pty Ltd.,
P.O. Box 704, Windsor, NSW 2756 Australia

If you have questions or comments about this book, please contact:
Lark Books
67 Broadway
Asheville, NC 28801
(828) 253-0467
Manufactured In China

ISBN 1-57990-369-X

table of contents

what makes

When you think of a garden, do you envision roses and holly-hocks nodding by a cottage door or neat rows of vegetables in an outdoor plot? Who said a garden had to be big or that it even had to be outdoors? If you've ever yearned to create a garden of your own but thought you didn't have the time or real estate to create one, yearn no longer! Whether you're an apartment dweller or you'd sim-ply rather spend more time admiring a garden than tilling and spading and weeding,

Beautiful Tabletop Gardens shows you how to create more than 30 gorgeous, easy-to-make gardens, all specially designed and sized to sit on a tabletop and to flourish indoors.

If you're looking for instant gratification, this book is full of lovely and unusual gardens assembled from plants and materials easily purchased at nurseries and home improve-ment centers. But if speed isn't important and you're attracted to the process of creating gar-dens from cuttings or by forc-ing bulbs to flower, you'll also find many projects that incorpo-

rate those techniques or high-light the growth process itself. Start now to make the spectac-ular Living Succulent Table Wreath (page 123) in time for the holidays, or learn how to force bulbs during winter so you can watch the happy faces of spring unfurl in the Daffodil Dish Garden (page 113).

Some projects in this book let you have your garden and eat it, too! Assemble a Loft Herb Garden (page 38) or a trio of Pick-Your-Own Salad Gardens (page 35). Plant vividly colored nursery starts of lettuce, broc-coli, cabbage, and edible flowers

a garden?

and keep them handy on the dinner table so you can pinch some off for your salad whenever you want. These gardens make great gifts, too. Any friend would be delighted to receive the Victorian Flower Message Garden (page 56) as a hand-made message from the heart.

Are you attracted to the off-beat? It's easier than you'd think to assemble your own tabletop Bog Garden from plants you'd normally find in a swamp or lagoon. See page 48 for directions. (Hint: Find your old Tupperware.) Or go the other direction and make a Zen Sand Garden—yes, mostly from

sand—to help you contemplate the inner you. Try making a pair of Lichen Topiaries (page 70) that put a fun, contemporary twist on the old boxwood standards. In short, the gardens in this book are about as far as you can get from grandma's dusty rubber plant or the usual pot of geraniums in a kitchen window.

Beautiful Tabletop Gardens will also teach you how to select healthy plants and prepare containers for your gardens. Learn tried-and-true techniques for potting and planting, and how to provide your gardens with the light, water, and food they need, plus a few special consid-

erations because they live indoors. Did you know, for example, that during winter-time, the air in the average living room is as dry as the Sahara Desert's? (Plants hate that.) Or that, given a choice, most indoor gardens would prefer a consistently cool room over a warm one? Illustrated charts will also help you recognize any potential problems and take corrective action to keep your gardens at their best.

Just about anyone can grow a garden successfully, one table-top at a time. *Beautiful Tabletop Gardens* will show you how.

the basics

Chapter 1

Tabletop gardens have the same needs as any plant: good soil and the right amounts of light, water, and fertilizer. In addition, your gardens will have a few easy-to-provide special needs: adequately sized containers, proper drainage, more humidity than the average indoor environment, and protection from extreme changes in temperature. If you pay regular attention to these basics, your gardens will flourish. But instead of being a chore, pottering about the garden (even a tabletop-sized one) is one of the joys of gardening, isn't it?

The information below helps your gardens get a good start and stay healthy, but there's no substitute for looking at them carefully on a regular basis—while you're savoring your morning cup of coffee, perhaps. See page 22 for important indicators of your garden's health—or its incipient problems.

Choosing Plants and Containers

Do you like starting completely from scratch? If you're going to grow a garden from seed, check the seed packets for growing instructions and make sure they fall within the suggested expiration date, since the germination rate of seed decreases with age. If you buy ready-grown plants or nursery starts, review the charts on pages 22 through 25 first so you'll be able to recognize unhealthy plants or identify those infested with bugs.

What's in a Name? Understanding the Names of Plants

This book gives both the common and botanical names of the plants used in each tabletop

garden, and nursery plants may be labelled either or both ways. Here's how to understand the terminology: First of all, a plant may be known among gardeners only by its scientific name, such as coleus, impatiens, or philodendron. Or, it may not have a common name or it may have more than one. For example, the plant known as coral bells, used in one of the Phases of the Moon Gardens (page 31) may also be called alum root. Its botanical name is *Heuchera americana* 'Pewter Moon.' Heuchera is the genus, and functions much like a person's surname—the Doe in John Doe, for example. *Americana* is a

species, or variation, within the *Heuchera* genus (John, as opposed to his brother Bob, Doe). This particular variety of *Heuchera* is a cultivar named 'Pewter Moon,' and it was created through cultivation, not in the wild. Cultivar names generally aren't written in Latin.

Preparing Containers and Planting the Garden

The how-to projects amply demonstrate how creative you can be in choosing containers for tabletop gardens. The technique described on page 14 of "planting" a garden with plants that remain in their original pots is useful when you're working with an unusual container. If, on the other hand, you want to plant a garden directly inside a terra-cotta container, soak the empty container overnight in water, so its porous material won't wick

away moisture from the garden. If planting in a previously used pot, sterilize any lingering diseases by soaking the pot in a chlorine-bleach-and-water solution (one part bleach to nine parts water), then rinse with lots of water.

Cover the bottom of the pot with a layer of charcoal, broken crockery, or gravel (If your container doesn't have a drainage hole, this step is critical). Bags of chipped or pulverized charcoal are available at garden centers. Add a shallow layer of potting compost or potting soil.

If any of the plants are pot bound, gently loosen the matted roots, then position them on the compost layer. Fill the container with more soil, firming it and bringing it up to the bottom of the plants' stems (but no higher than 1/2 inch [1.3 cm] beneath the rim of the container, to allow room for watering). Tap the pot against the table to further settle the soil. If you're planting rooted cuttings, use the pointed tool called a *dibber* (or another suitably shaped tool) to make a hole in the soil. Insert the rooted end into the hole and gently firm the soil around it. Water the garden carefully and thoroughly. Keep

it well-misted and in a shady spot about a week to avoid "plant shock" and wilting, then move it to its intended tabletop.

The roots of plants in a tabletop garden ultimately intertwine, so if you think you might like to change some out at a later date, keep the plants in their individual pots and "plant" them in a larger container (see below).

Water the plants well, at least an hour before planting. With the fingers of your opposing hand spread over the soil surface, gently invert the plant, dislodging it by running a knife around the rim or rapping it against a table if necessary.

"Planting" with Potted Plants

The gardens in this book have been designed to incorporate plants with the same basic needs. For example, you wouldn't expect to successfully combine a desert cactus and moisture-loving ferns, would you? Their needs for upkeep are simply too different.

However, if you decide to modify a garden design and absolutely must use plants with different water needs, keep the plants in individual pots,

position them inside a larger container filled with peat, and fill in the spaces between pots, covering the surface with more peat if necessary. Then use a watering can with a long spout to water the plants per their individual needs. The peat can also be kept moist to raise humidity levels; see page 20.

How to Work with Cuttings

Two of the projects in this book are great for learning how to propagate cuttings from "mother" plants. For information on how to make cuttings from plants that root easily in water, refer to the Tabletop Cutting Garden on page 118. To make

cuttings from succulent plants (which actually suffer if they're too wet), see the Living Succulent Tabletop Wreath on page 123. You'll also learn a bit about pruning in the Rosemary Topiaries project on page 70.

Bulb-Based Gardens

Gardens created from bulbs, such as the Daffodil Dish Garden (page 113) have their own fascinations and requirements, and they're a great way to create blooming gardens indoors during the winter months. The key is to trick the bulbs, which normally flower in springtime, by planting them in a container and pre-cooling them a certain amount of time in a cold, dark place such as an unheated basement or the refrigerator, maintaining a temperature of 40 to 50°F (4 to 10°C). The cooling period mimics the low temperatures a bulb normally would experience overwintering in the ground. See the chart at right for the cooling requirements of different bulbs. Protect refrigerated bulbs from vegetables and fruit, which naturally emit a gas that impedes flowering.

Cooling Periods for Forced Bulbs

Crocus *(Iridaceae)*	8 to 10 weeks
Narcissus/Daffodil *(Amaryllidaceae)*	12 to 15 weeks
Hyacinth *(Hyacinthus)*	12 to 15 weeks
Iris *(Iridaceae)*	10 to 14 weeks
Lily of the Valley *(Convallaria)*	10 to 12 weeks
Muscari/Grape Hyacinth *(Liliaceae)*	10 to 14 weeks
Tulip *(Tulipa)*	12 to 16 weeks

To force bulbs, you may wish to use a low, flat container specially designed for that purpose. Prepare the container with layers of gravel and soil and add the bulbs, root ends down, pointed ends up, spaced apart, not touching the pot sides. Cover with potting compost and water well. Make a note of the planting date, and put the garden in cold storage, checking it weekly to make sure the soil is moist but not sodden.

After the specified cooling time and after the bulbs have produced roots about 2 inches (5 cm) long, put the container in a cool location with bright, indirect light. You'll have blooms in a few weeks! Keep the garden well-watered and away from heat and direct sunlight for maximum flowering time.

Crocuses and hyacinths also can be forced and flourish in containers filled with water, not soil. Put the bulbs in paper bags and cool them as specified in the chart on page 15, at temperatures between 50 to 55°F (10 to 12°C). Then place the bulbs, root ends down, in a pebble-filled, watertight container or in individual glass forcing vases. Fill the containers with enough water so the water just touches the bottom of the bulbs. Put the bulbs in a cool, dark location, adding more water as needed, until the roots are 2 inches (5 cm) long. Then move them to a cool, indirectly lit location and you'll have blooms in about two weeks. Forced bulbs can't be forced again, but their spectacular winter display makes the effort worth it!

Soil

As tempting as it may be to fill your container with earth from your yard, don't! (Unless you'll also enjoy the challenge of combating diseases and pests you import inside.) Instead, use potting soil or soilless growing medium sold by the bag at garden centers. Note that soilless medium is a very light, peat-based mixture which needs to be kept watered and not allowed to dry out; if your tabletop garden has a top-heavy design, add sand to the medium and/or use a heavy container as a counterbalance.

When buying soil, pay attention to the labelling and how it matches the requirements of the tabletop garden you'd like to make. Some potting soils contain added nutrients or a richer proportion of compost to give plants a boost, but the herbs in the Loft Herb Garden (page 38), for example, perform better in hardier soil. Also, if you're planting a garden during the dormant winter season, you don't want to "feed" the transplants by putting them in extra-rich soil. Soils specifically created for specialty plants, such as orchids, cacti, or lime-averse plants, such as cyclamen, are also available.

Food

Being indoors, your tabletop garden can't derive nutrients from the outdoor ecosystem, which provides nourishment via organic elements returning to the soil. After a couple of months, the nutrients in the container will be exhausted, and you'll need to keep the garden fertilized during its periods of active growth. But beware of overfeeding; you may stunt their growth or scorch the leaves. Withhold fertilizer during the months of fall and winter dormancy, unless the garden comprises plants that bloom in those seasons.

Water-soluble fertilizers in liquid or powder form are best for several reasons. Every other time you water, use a fertilizer-and-water solution mixed weaker than the manufacturer recommends. This gets the nutrients down deep, where the roots can immediately absorb them without the risk of over-fertilization. Fertilizer in stick or granular form, on the other hand, may penetrate the soil only to an undesirably shallow depth or may continue to release nutrients when the garden's dormant period starts (also bad).

For an authentic touch, do as farmers do in the spring: After removing a shallow layer of the old dirt on the top, top-dress your tabletop garden with fresh potting compost. Be careful not to injure roots.

other foliage or flowering plants. Mature plants need more than rooted cuttings. The larger the plants' leaves or the faster their growth, the greater the need for water. Plants need less water during their dormant periods: around one to three waterings a month and barely that for cacti and succulents. If a garden is in a hot location with low humidity, however, expect to water it more frequently. Gardens in pots made of clay or other "breathable" materials also need more frequent watering. See the chart on page 24 for clues your garden can give you to its water needs.

Barring the Bog Garden and Water Garden (pages 48 and 51), most of the gardens in this

Water

Your tabletop gardens have two separate issues regarding water: the amount of water they need and their ambient humidity, i.e., how much water is in the air around them.

Three factors affect water needs: the type of plants, the season, and the immediate environs. Thick-leaved succulents and cacti require much less water compared to most

book prefer the moist/dry watering treatment, which also encourages their roots to grow deeply into the soil. Frequently dribbling a little water on the garden is not recommended! Instead, water until the soil is moist, then let dry until the top 1/2 inch (1.3 cm) of soil is dry to the touch; check by using a finger to dig into the soil without injuring any roots. Succulents should be treated the same way all year except during their dormant winter season when the soil should be allowed to

almost dry out. The soil of flowering plants other than succulents, however, should be kept evenly moist but not saturated.

Watering Techniques

If you really want to pamper your gardens, collect fresh rainwater or use tepid, not cold, tap water that you let stand overnight (to disperse some of the chlorine). Using a watering can with a long, thin spout, pour water directly on the soil without wetting the leaves, until water starts to drain from the bottom. After 30 minutes, pour away any excess water in the drip dish; roots can't breathe underwater! If the container has no drainage hole, water bit by bit. Never leave plants standing in slushy soil; pour off any excess.

If your garden's container has a drainage hole or the plants' leaves react badly to direct contact with water (true for begonias and gloxinias), use the immersion method. Lower the container into a sink filled with water, to a point just below the level of the soil in the container. Let it sit until the plants have drawn up enough water through the drainage hole to moisten the surface of the soil. Remove from the water and let drain, then return the garden to its desired location.

"Hard" water (i.e., water that's high in mineral content) may eventually cause a crust to form on top of the soil; it's harmless. Use a fork or small trowel to scratch it up and keep the soil aerated.

Maintaining Humidity

A very moist environment with little fresh air is a breeding ground for plant diseases, such as botrytis, a gray mold disease caused by a fungus that's highly destructive to flowering plants. But on the other hand, most plants flourish in air moister than indoor environments typically provide. A centrally heated room in winter may literally have the humidity of a desert. Air conditioners also decrease humidity, although cool air holds more water than warm air. Ideal relative humidity falls within a 40 to 60 percent range. You can use a tool called a *hygrometer* (available at garden centers) to measure a room's humidity.

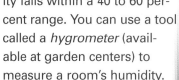

POTTING AND PLANTING SUPPLIES: GOOD THINGS TO HAVE FOR INDOOR GARDENING

tools and implements

hand trowel

kitchen fork

dibber or another pointed tool

pruning shears

scissors

watering can

clean spray bottle

hygrometer

minimum/maximum thermometer

compass

materials

containers of your choice

gravel, chipped or pulverized charcoal, or broken crockery

potting compost

potting soil

soilless growing medium

dried moss*

bagged peat

water-soluble plant food in liquid or powder form

*Available in bagged and sheet form at craft and floral supply stores

optional but nice to have

bulb forcing container

paper bags

sand

small, clean pebbles

chlorine bleach

*See page 14 for how to create a bleach-and-water solution to sterilize used pots.

Fresh air ventilation lowers the temperature but it also lowers humidity. Grouping plants, as these tabletop gardens do, raises humidity by trapping air between leaves (good), but don't cram them so closely that air circulation is blocked (bad). Use a garden hose fitted with an adjustable mister nozzle or a spray bottle, to mist plants with water in the early morning when it's cool. That way, they can dry before direct sunlight hits the leaves. Or, try double potting: Fill your garden's decorative container with peat, "plant" it with plants still in their individual pots, then keep the peat continually moist.

Many experts recommend a pebble tray. Fill a waterproof, 2-inch-deep (5 cm) tray with an inch-thick (2.5 cm) layer of pebbles or gravel. Add water until it rises halfway up the pebbles, and set the garden on top. Add more water to the tray as needed.

Temperature and Light

Most indoor gardens live quite happily in the range of 60 to 75°F (15 to 23°C) and during their dormant winter phase, tolerate even lower temperatures. With the exception of some flowering plants which need a specific number of cool nights to bloom, and cacti and succulents, which evolved to tolerate climactic extremes, plants are most seriously affected by dramatic drops in temperature, i.e.,15 degrees or greater. If you're a fresh air fiend who keeps windows open at night, even in winter, move plants to protected locations. Don't allow drafts (strong, sustained air currents) to pass over the plants, either (although the Sensory Grass Garden on page 80 is designed for breezes). Use a minimum/maximum thermometer, available at home improvement stores, to determine typical temperature variations.

As a very general rule of thumb, indoor plants do best in a cool, sunny location. Your gardens' need for light can be more specifically assessed in two ways: the amount, i.e., the number of hours of sunlight it receives per day, and the intensity, how bright the light is. Also bear in mind that sunlight's

intensity falls off dramatically the further a garden is from a window, so keep an eye on your garden for signs that it's getting too little sun (refer to the chart on page 24 for clues).

The Terminology of Sunlight

What does it mean when a nursery plant is marked, "Does best in semi-shade," or, "Full sun only?" Here are the terms most frequently used:

•Full Sun: Locate plant within 2 feet (61 cm) of a southern exposure where sun falls directly on leaves. Even these plants may need light shade at midday, perhaps provided by a window sheer or blind. Cacti, succulents, and geraniums grow best here.

•Some Direct Sun: Bright light, with direct sun on the leaves part of the day. Near, but no closer than 2 feet (61 cm) to a southern exposure or within 2 feet of window with eastern or western exposure.

•Bright but Sunless: Within 5 feet (1.5 m) of a sunny window, but no sun falls directly on leaves.

•Semi-shade: Within 5 to 8 feet (1.5 to 2.4 m) of a sunny window or close to a sunless window. Good for foliage, not recommended for flowering plants.

•Shade: Poorly lit, but you could still read a book using only natural light during a 3- to 4-hour period.

Exposure

Buy a compass to help you determine the exposures of all the windows in your home and therefore the type of sunlight each receives. A window that faces south is said to have a southern exposure, and the same applies to the other compass directions:

•Southern: The brightest light and the longest period of direct sun. Hot and dry location. Leaf burn potential. Position bright-light plants a few feet from a southern window.

•Northern: Indirect light, cool location. Good for foliage plants but don't expect flowers to be happy there.

•Eastern: If you have only eastern-facing windows, consider yourself lucky! The morning sun will be bright but cool, and the afternoon light indirect. Good for plants that need a limited amount of direct sun without the intensity of a southern exposure or the heat of a western exposure (see below).

•Western: Direct light in the afternoon and the hottest sunlight. Be careful what you put here, conditions are hot and dry. How much do you like cactus?

Keeping Your Gardens Healthy

Assuming you've planted your gardens in the right container and you're providing the basics of proper light, water, drainage, food, and air, the best way to keep your tabletop gardens healthy is literally to keep an eye on them. Check them on a regular basis. Study the charts starting on the next page so you'll be able to recognize common problems and take quick remedial action.

Common Indoor Diseases and Pests (and How to Get Rid of Them)

Avoiding problems starts at the nursery. Study the information below, then select plants with healthy growth and lots of buds (if they're flowering varieties). Before replanting, sterilize the garden containers if possible (page 14). Then, if you really pay attention to the basics of keeping your gardens healthy, they'll be much more resistant to disease and pests. In fact, that's a key element of organic farming.

If bugs appear, forget about using a pesticide indoors; it's too toxic. Working outside, in a bathtub or shower stall, or on the kitchen counter, spray the garden with an insecticidal soap or a homemade soap-and-water solution (1 gallon [3.8 L] of warm water combined with 1 tablespoon [15 mL] of mild dishwashing liquid). To ward off bugs, some gardeners also steep dried chile peppers or crushed garlic in water, then spray it on.

If foliage becomes diseased, pick off the affected leaves and apply a sulfur-based, organic fungicide (available at garden centers). See the chart below for more information on common problems and solutions.

Diseases

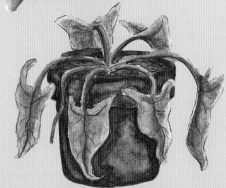

Sooty Mold

Sooty Mold

A black mold on leaves that interferes with chlorophyll production

Solutions

Spray with insectidal soap or homemade soap-and-water solution (see above)

Wipe with a paper towel or cotton square saturated with rubbing alcohol

Powdery Mildew

Powdery Mildew

White or gray patches of fungus that appear on leaves and flowers, causing them to eventually discolor and fall off. When treating powdery mildew, wash your hands before touching healthy parts of a plant—or other plants—or you'll spread it

Solutions

Spray plant with a solution made by mixing 1 gallon (3.8 mL) of warm water, 5 tablespoons (75 mL) of liquid antiseptic soap, and 3 tablespoons (45 mL) of baking soda

Stem and Crown Rot

Stem and Crown Rot

Due to overwatering, poor air circulation, or inadequate drainage, stems and roots are attacked by a fungus and turn mushy

Solutions

Trimming away problem areas usually fails. Throw away the whole plant and start over

Pests

Whiteflies

When an affected plant is shaken, clouds of these small, mothlike insects fly up from the undersides of leaves, where they hide. They suck plant juices and excrete a sticky substance called honeydew, which can cause distorted growth. Leaves will become discolored and eventually fall

Solutions

Wipe the undersides of leaves with soapy water or rubbing solution (do this at night when the whiteflies are at rest)

Suck the insects off with a handheld vacuum cleaner

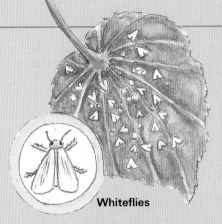
Whiteflies

Red Spider Mites

Tiny, six-legged, sap-sucking insects that can be detected by the webbing they leave on the underside of leaves. Mottled, pale yellow, and falling leaves are also a clue

Solution

Knock them off with a strong spray of water

Spray with insecticidal soap or homemade soap-and-water solution (page 22)

Prune away infested areas

Red Spider Mites

Scale

Sap-sucking, honeydew-excreting insects that look like flat, brown, oval bumps. Plant leaves yellow and fall off

Solutions

Scrape or scrub them off, using soapy water and a cloth or small brush (toothbrush size is good)

Scale

Mealybugs

Sap-sucking, honeydew-excreting insects identified by their white, fluffy, cottonlike exteriors. Often found at the joins between plant stem and leaves, which are deformed or yellow

Solutions

Same as for Sooty Mold (see above)

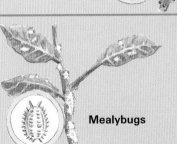
Mealybugs

Aphids

Sap-sucking, honeydew-excreting insects with soft, usually green bodies (although they can also be clear, black, brown, orange, red, or white)

Solutions

Pick off by hand or knock off with a strong spray of water

Spray with insecticidal soap or homemade soap-and-water solution (page 22)

Aphids

Too Much or Too Little?
Your Plants Can Tell You What They Want

The charts below help you to interpret "plantspeak." They contain valuable clues to help you keep your tabletop gardens healthy. While you water and groom your gardens, keep an eye on the foliage, flowers, and even the soil for changes that are sudden, differ from the norm, or are out of season (leaves falling off in the spring, for example). Take corrective action as necessary.

Light

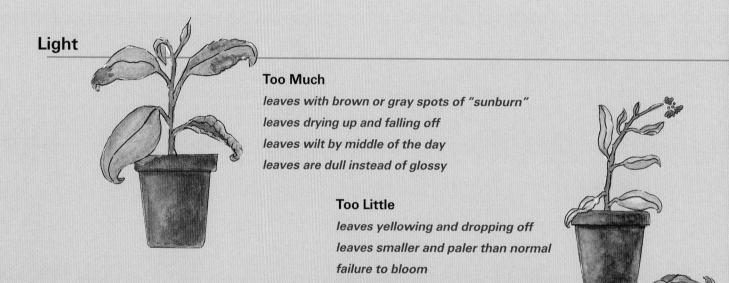

Too Much

leaves with brown or gray spots of "sunburn"

leaves drying up and falling off

leaves wilt by middle of the day

leaves are dull instead of glossy

Too Little

leaves yellowing and dropping off

leaves smaller and paler than normal

failure to bloom

lower leaves yellow, wither, and fall off

spindly growth with too much space between leaves

normally variegated leaves are solid green in color

Water

Too Much

leaves become limp and develop soft, rotten areas

leaves yellow, curl, and wilt

leaf tips turn brown

brown, mushy roots

both young and mature leaves drop off

mold appears on flowers

Too Little

mature leaves fall off

flowers quickly fade and fall off

leaf edges turn brown and dry

lower leaves curl, yellow, and wilt

Humidity

Too Much

mold on leaves or flowers

patches of rot on leaves or stems

Too Little

brown, shrivelled leaf tips

leaves wilt or develop yellow edges

flowers or buds shrivel and fall off

leaves fall off

Food

Too Much

growth stunted

leaves wilt or develop scorched edges and brown, dry spots

a whitish crust appears on soil surface or pot (and you're in a soft-water area)

Temperature

Too Warm

flowers don't last

spindly growth, although plants are in good light

lower leaves develop brown edges or wilt

leaves at bottom fall off

Too Cold

leaves curl, brown, and fall off

Extreme Change in Temperature

leaves quickly turn yellow and fall off

Too Little

tendency to manifest diseases or infestations by pests

pale or unnaturally spotted leaves

small, poorly colored, or absent flowers

droopy stems

lower leaves prematurely fall

earth, water, air, sky

Chapter 2

These gardens bring the outdoors inside in table-size tableaux, highlighting the basic elements. Float aquatic plants in a superb tabletop Water Garden, or amuse dinner guests by decorating the table with precisely sheared Time to Cut the Grass Gardens.

easy succulent table gardens

Succulents have to be among the easiest indoor plants to care for. Simply give them bright sunlight, good drainage, and fresh air. The close spacing of the plants in these gardens and their color coordination with the mottled gray containers create a quietly luxurious effect.

blue echeveria *(Echeveria glauca)*

Plants

pig's ear or round-leaf navel wort *(Cotyledon orbiculata)*

burro's tail *(Sedum morganianum)*

Gasteria maculata

blue echeveria *(Echeveria glauca)*

Gasteria maculata

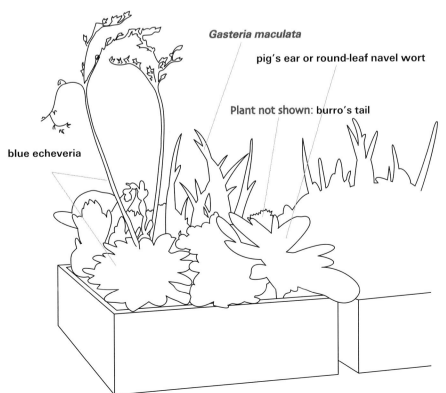

Gasteria maculata

pig's ear or round-leaf navel wort

Plant not shown: burro's tail

blue echeveria

pig's ear or round-leaf navel wort *(Cotyledon orbiculata)*

Tools and Materials

2 square containers, wood or pottery, each about 12 inches (30.5 cm) square

newspaper

gray, dark blue or purple, white, and black acrylic craft paint

1-inch (2.5 cm) paintbrush

sea sponge

2 plastic liners, sized to fit inside the containers

potting and planting supplies listed on page 20

1. Place the containers on the newspaper and paint them gray. Let dry, then use the sponge to dab and stroke on the white, blue or purple, and black paints unevenly and very sparingly to achieve the effect shown in the photograph. Let dry.

2. Arrange the plants in the plastic liners after preparing each one with a bottom layer of drainage material, then potting soil. Fill in any spaces with more potting soil.

3. Lower a plant-filled liner into each container, and place the containers in a spot that gets some direct sunlight every day (but avoid letting them burn in summer). Misting is not required; water when the soil dries out. During the dormant season, keep in a cool area and water only once every one to two months. Blooms on the blue echeveria last for months and can be snipped off when blooming has finished or left on to ripen seeds.

phases of the moon gardens

Waxing and waning, light and dark . . . These two gardens are effective in moonlight or any dramatically lit setting. The white garden features white, silver, and pale green colors, including lychnis, which produces small, pinkish-white spring flowers, and Dutch lavender, which produces blue flowers in summer. The purple and green plants of the dark garden include coral bells, which flowers white in spring. Blown glass ornaments and iridescent pebbles add extra drama.

White Garden

Plants

wormwood *(Artemisia 'Powis Castle')*

dusty miller *(Senecio vira-vira)*

lamb's ears *(Stachys byzantina 'Silver Carpet')*

rosemary *(Rosmarinus officinalis)*

sage, mixed types *(Salvia berggarten and S. tricolor)*

lychnis 'Angel Blush' *(Lychnis coronaria 'Angel Blush')*

Dutch lavender *(Lavandula intermedia 'Dutch')*

Gynura **'Purple Passion'***

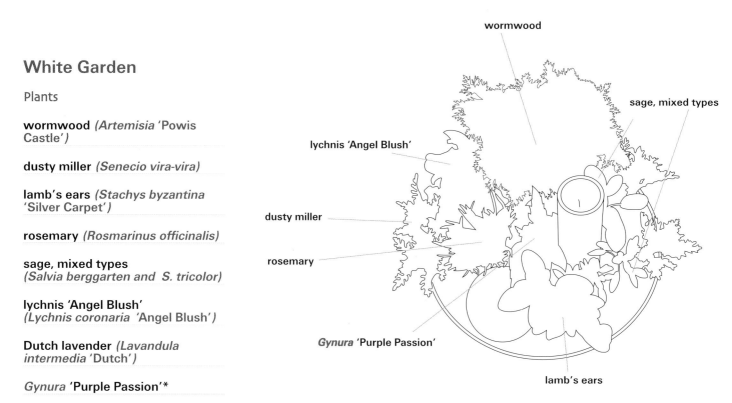

wormwood

sage, mixed types

lychnis 'Angel Blush'

dusty miller

rosemary

Gynura 'Purple Passion'

lamb's ears

lamb's ears *(Stachys byzantina 'Silver Carpet')*

wormwood *(Artemisia 'Powis Castle')*

purple passion *(Gynura)*

Dark Garden

Plants

sweet potato vine *(Ipomoea batatas)*

coral bells, also known as alum root
(Heuchera 'Silver Scrolls'*)*

Leea guineensis 'Purple Desire' *

Hemigraphis alternata 'Purple Waffle' *

*If your local nursery doesn't carry these, they can be purchased from tropical plant retailers on the Internet.

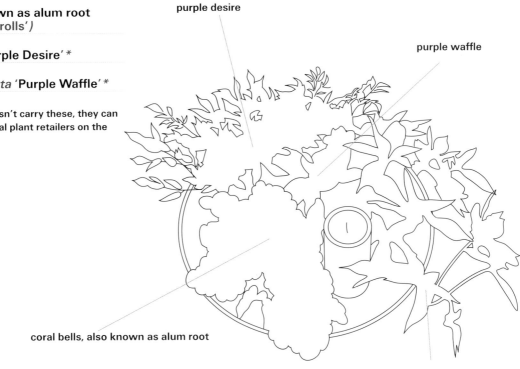

purple desire

purple waffle

coral bells, also known as alum root

sweet potato vine

sweet potato vine *(Ipomoea batatas)*

coral bells, also known as alum root *(Heuchera* 'Silver Scrolls'*)*

Leea guineensis 'Purple Desire'

Hemigraphis alternata 'Purple Waffle'

Tools and Materials

2 large plastic salad bowls, 18 inches (46.7 cm) in diameter

2 plastic plates, dinner size (optional)

masking tape (optional)

power drill and 1/4-inch (6 mm) drill bit (optional)

helpful friend

alcohol

clean rags

newspaper

silver chrome spray paint

potting and planting supplies listed on page 20

large blown-glass ornament or float

iridescent glass pebbles*

2 pillar candles (optional)

*Available at craft stores

1. If desired, add drainage holes to the bowls and plan to add the dinner plates as drainage saucers. Invert a bowl so it's upside down and affix a piece of masking tape at the centerpoint of the bottom. While your friend holds the bowl firmly in place on a work surface, drill a hole. Remove the tape. Repeat with the other bowl.

2. Use the alcohol and rags to clean the bowls and plates of any dirt and oil. Set them on newspaper and spray-paint. Let dry.

3. Plant the gardens, as shown on pages 32 and 33. Add the glass ornaments and iridescent pebbles to cover any exposed soil. Place them (on top of the dinner plates, if necessary) in an area that receives direct sun. For extra nighttime drama, add a pillar candle to each garden if desired.

pick-your-own
garden salad

Many people don't realize how easy it is to buy vegetable starts at a nursery and to grow those starts indoors in a sunny spot. As well as harvesting the lettuces, you can pinch off the young leaves of cruciferous veggies, such as broccoli and cabbage, to add taste and nutrition to your dinner salads. Or, enjoy their gorgeous colors and textures even if you never pick a leaf.

Plants

red Swiss chard (*Beta vulgaris*), in half-grown and baby sizes

red and green lettuces (*Lactuca sativa* 'Red Sails' and *L. sativa* 'Black Seeded Simpson' or other varieties)

garden nasturtium (*Tropaeolum majus*)

broccoli (*Brassica oleracea* 'Early Emerald' or another variety)

cabbage (*Brassica oleracea Capitata* 'Stonehead' or another variety)

kale (*Brassica oleracea Acephala* 'Blue Curled Scotch' or another variety)

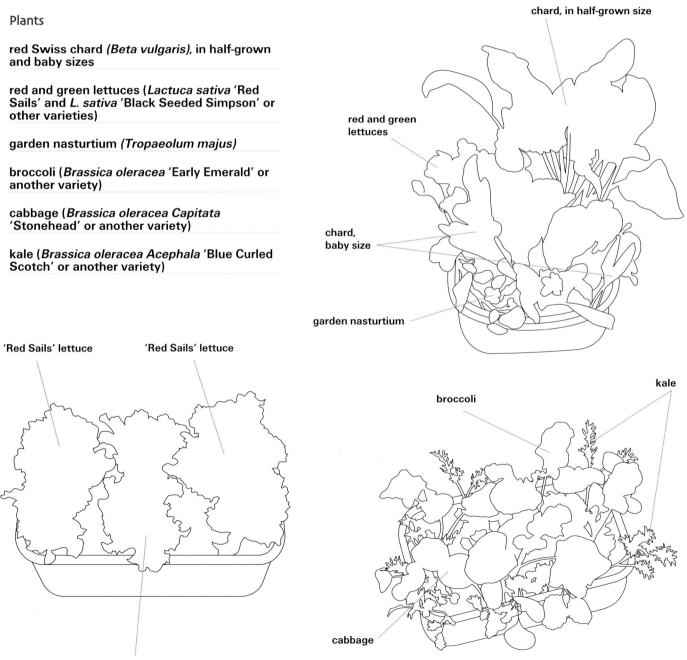

chard, in half-grown size

red and green lettuces

chard, baby size

garden nasturtium

'Red Sails' lettuce

'Red Sails' lettuce

'Black Seeded Simpson' lettuce

broccoli

kale

cabbage

Tools and Materials

three leakproof metal containers, enamelled or galvanized*

potting and planting supplies listed on page 20

*Vintage pans like those shown in the photographs can be found at flea markets and junk shops.

1. The key to this garden is to plant the contrasting colors of the chard and lettuces in simple, graphic patterns. Follow the instructions for adding gravel and soil to the containers (page 14).

2. Working with the tall chard, plant one end of the largest container, working on the diagonal. Follow it with a row of the green lettuce, then a row of the chard starts. Finish with the nasturtiums for a nice contrast of orange blossoms against the purple-red of the chard.

3. Plant the red and green lettuces in the second container, forming three contrasting rows of color. Fill the third container with the broccoli and cabbage starts placed randomly; underplant them with the smaller kale starts.

4. Keep the gardens well-watered in a spot that gets lots of bright, indirect light.

loft herb garden

A garden in a long, low planter goes perfectly with the clean, industrial look of loft apartments. This kind of container also helps each plant get an even amount of light. Pick among the herbs listed below, or go wild and plant them all! Keep your herb garden at hand in the kitchen, so you can enjoy the herbs' wonderful aromas and harvest what you need as you cook.

Plants

lemon verbena *(Aloysia triphylla)*

catnip *(Nepeta cataria)*

common thyme *(Thymus vulgaris)*

oregano *(Origanum vulgare* 'Jim Best' *or another variety)*

rosemary *(Rosmarinus officinalis)*

basil *(Ocimum basilicum,* 'Spicy Globe,' 'Miniature,' *or another variety)*

tricolor or gold sage *(Salvia officinalis)*

chives *(Allium schoenoprasum)*

lemon verbena *(Aloysia triphylla)*

basil *(Ocimum basilicum, either* 'Spicy Globe' *or* 'Miniature'*)*

oregano *(Origanum vulgare* 'Jim Best'*)*

rosemary *(Rosmarinus officinalis)*

Tools and Materials

simple rectangular container, about 7 inches (17.8 cm) high and 40 inches (101.6 cm) long

potting and planting supplies listed on page 20

plant markers (optional)

fine-tip permanent marker (optional)

1. Fill the container with a layer of drainage material and 6 inches (15.2 cm) of potting soil that's rather plain and not too rich in nutrients. Herbs prefer a hardier soil, with an occasional feeding of liquid fertilizer.

2. Plant the herbs, spacing them evenly and adding plant markers, if desired, to help you remember which is which. From left to right, the herbs shown in the photograph on page 38 are basil, rosemary, oregano, thyme, catnip, and verbena.

3. Set the garden where it will get as much direct sun as possible and give it enough water to prevent wilting, i.e., don't drown the herbs. When the herbs begin to flower, pinch off the blossoms to encourage leaf growth and to keep them from getting too leggy.

herbal tea garden

This "teapot" features essential herbs that love full sun, and you can use any of them to make delicious herbal teas. Did you know that common bee balm, often found growing wild, is part of the recipe for making the world-famous tea called Earl Grey? Grown on a wire form that's stuffed with moss and soil, the herbs in this garden can be picked and immediately steeped in hot water to a strength you prefer.

spearmint *(Mentha spicata)*

Plants

assorted thymes: lemon thyme *(Thymus citriodorus)*, creeping thyme *(T. praecox arcticus)*, silver or wooly thyme *(T. lanuginosus)*, or common thyme *(T. vulgaris)*

lemon balm *(Melissa officinalis)*

bee balm *(Monarda didyma)*

corsican mint *(Mentha requienii)*

spearmint *(Mentha spicata)*

lemon thyme *(Thymus citriodorus)*

Materials and Supplies

wire form in the shape of a teapot

potting and planting supplies listed on page 20

dried moss

drainage saucer

1. Put a little moss inside the spout, handle, and/or lid of the wire teapot, poking soil in the middle to form an earthen center. Planting these areas with small-leaf herbs, such as corsican mint and thymes, helps give more definition to these areas.

2. Tease the plants through the wire, making sure their roots go into the soil core. To make the job easier, you may have to "bareroot" the plants first, removing the dirt from the root ball while leaving long roots essentially intact. One way to do this is to use a garden hose with a pressure nozzle that produces a high-pressure, low-volume stream of water.

3. Very loosely line the bottom third of the wire form with the dried moss, then add a layer of potting soil, patting it gently so it conforms to the shape of the form.

4. Repeat steps 2 and 3 to plant the next third of the pot, then the final third, grouping or alternating the herbs as desired.

5. Place the teapot on the drainage saucer in a sunny location and keep it well-watered. Tea, anyone?

time to cut the grass gardens

The key to the decorative impact of these simple grass gardens is the contrast between the absolute precision of their sheared tops and the intertwined moss in the containers. Very simple gardens like these look absolutely stunning when they're used in multiples, too. Position them in a line down the middle of the table for a dinner party and give each guest one to take home.

Plants

ornamental blue fescue or another variety of grass in 1-gallon (3.8L) containers

ornamental blue fescue

Tools and Materials

glass containers*

small pebbles or gravel

large utility knife

dried moss

scissors

large hair comb (optional)

*The containers shown in the photograph are about the size of a gallon (3.8L) paint can.

1. Prepare each container by sprinkling a small amount of pebbles on the bottom for drainage. (You don't want them to be visible after the gardens are assembled.)

2. Unpot the fescue, and use the utility knife to size the root ball, making it slightly smaller than the glass container. Try to cut away an equal depth of the root ball around its circumference.

3. Wrap the root ball with dried moss and insert it into a container. Fill any gaps between the grass and the lip of the container with more moss.

4. Now it's time to give your gardens a haircut, using the scissors and keeping the blades horizontal relative to the grass. If you're really compulsive, play hairdresser by using the comb to separate the blades as you trim to achieve a level "top" to the garden.

5. Keep the gardens in a bright location, and water when the top of the soil feels dry.

easy cactus garden

Cactus gardens don't necessarily have to consist of bristly little pincushions in tiny pots. This free and easy garden combines two different kinds of cactus with a variety of beautifully shaped succulents that enjoy the same growing conditions.

Plants

string of hearts or rosary vine *(Ceropegia woodii)*

starfish cactus *(Stapelia grandiflora)*

variegated jade plant *(Portulacaria afra 'variegata')*

Christmas cactus *(Schlumbergera gaertneri)*

Sedum mexicanum

Tools and Materials

free-form ceramic planter*

drainage tray

potting and planting supplies listed on page 20

*The planter shown in the photograph is approximately 12 inches (30.5 cm) in diameter and 6 inches (15.2 cm) deep.

1. Put a layer of drainage material in the bottom of the planter and cover it with 2 to 3 inches (5 to 7.6 cm) of potting soil.

2. Plant the container according to the planting diagram below, filling in any gaps between the plants with more potting soil.

3. Place the garden in a location where it gets lots of bright light and a few hours of direct morning sun if possible. Water sparingly.

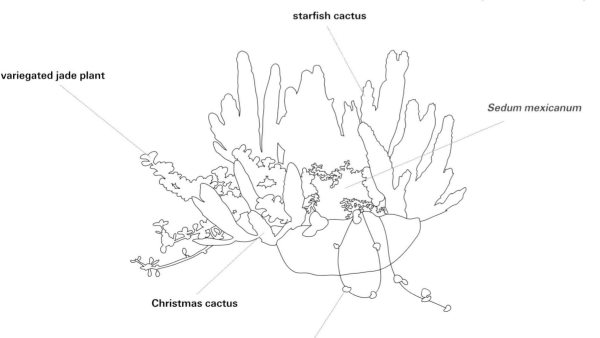

variegated jade plant

starfish cactus

Sedum mexicanum

Christmas cactus

string of hearts or rosary vine

bog garden

This tabletop bog garden is inventively housed in an old desk drawer lined with heavy plastic. Place the garden in an area that receives dappled sunlight. Keep the compost moist and the water containers filled, and mist the plants regularly.

water lettuce (*Pistia tratiotes*)

Plants

red pitcher plant *(Sarracenia leucophylla x purpurea)*

wavy rush *(Juncus effusus spiralis)*

miniature horsetail *(Equisetum scirpoides)*

water lettuce *(Pistia tratiotes)*

water hyacinth *(Eichhornia crassipes)*

fairy moss or feathered water fern *(Azolla pinnata)*

*Never dispose of this plant in a way that would allow it to breed in ponds, lakes, or other outdoor bodies of water, as it is considered a nuisance plant that interferes with oxygen production.

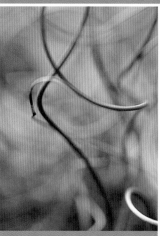
wavy rush
(*Juncus effusus spiralis*)

miniature horsetail
(*Equisetum scirpoides*)

water hyacinth
(*Eichhornia crassipes*)

red pitcher plant
(*Sarracenia leucophylla x purpurea*)

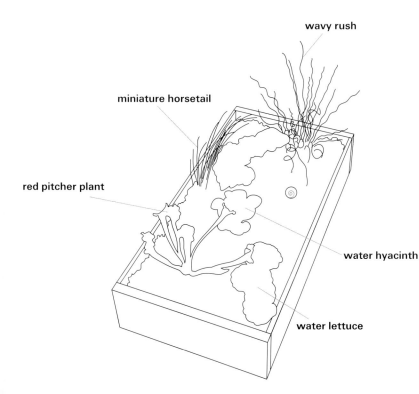
wavy rush

miniature horsetail

red pitcher plant

water hyacinth

water lettuce

Tools and Materials

desk drawer or other
rectangular wooden container

piece of heavy plastic sheeting
sized to line the bottom and
sides of the container

scissors

gravel

mushroom compost and other
potting and planting supplies
listed on page 20

small plastic food storage
containers

dried moss

1. The key to this garden's
design is the graceful placement of the plants within the
angular confines of the desk
drawer. Fit the plastic sheeting
inside the drawer, covering the
bottom and sides and folding
the corners neatly.

2. Put a layer of gravel in the
drawer and top it with a couple
of inches of compost. Make
three mounds of compost
where you wish to place the
pitcher plant and reeds. Put
them on the mounds.

3. Place the food storage
containers in the garden,
arranging them in a graceful
curve that connects the reeds.
Fill with water and add the lettuces and water hyacinth. Add a
pinch of the fairy moss to the
containers of water (it grows on
the surface).

4. Fill any remaining spaces
with more compost, and cover
the surface with moss, using it
to hide the edges of the plaster
or water containers.

water garden

You'll be surprised to learn of all the plants that can live happily in a tabletop water garden, which adds valuable humidity to the air. This project allows you to select plants that float and plants that are rooted under the waterline. Using several floating plants or a special dye for water gardens helps block sun rays and algae formation. Follow your local nursery's suggestions for locating the garden according to light needs, and try grouping plants of various sizes to make a big splash!

Plants

spiky, erect plants, such as papyrus *(Cyperus papyrus)*, sweet flag *(Acorus calamus)*, or yellow flag iris *(Iris pseudacorus)*

broad-leaf plants, such as giant arrowhead *(Sagittaria latifolia)* or calla lily *(Zantedeschia aethiopica)*

cascading plants, such as water mint *(Mentha aquatica)* or parrot feather *(Myriophyllum aquaticum)*

floating plants, such as water lettuce *(Pistia stratiotes)* or water hyacinth *(Eichhornia crassipes)*

surface plants, such as duckweed *(Lemnaceae)* and club moss *(Selaginella)*

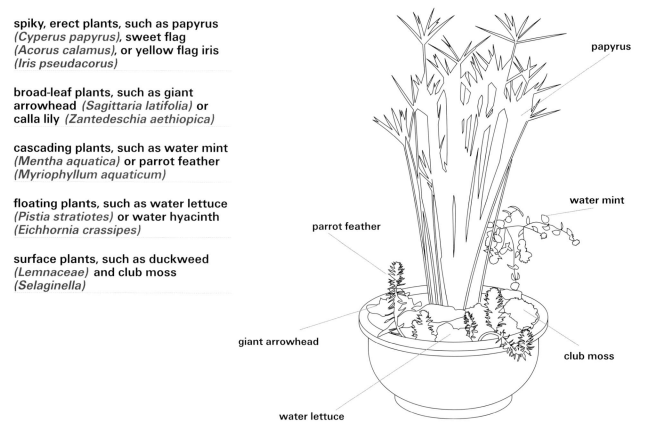

papyrus

water mint

parrot feather

giant arrowhead

club moss

water lettuce

papyrus *(Cyperus papyrus)*   parrot feather *(Myriophyllum aquaticum)*   water mint *(Mentha aquatica)*

Tools and Materials

glass container, 12 to 24 inches (30.5 to 61 cm)) wide and 12 to 16 inches (30.5 to 40.6 cm) deep*

small containers for plants rooted below the waterline, one per plant

heavy clay soil free of peat moss (a bit of sand is OK)

pebbles or tumbled glass chips

dye approved for water gardens (optional)

pulverized charcoal chips

water plant fertilizer (optional)

*The container's dimensions may vary. You may also use a waterproof plastic liner inside a ceramic container or basket.

1. Use the clay to pot the spiky and broad-leaf plants in the small containers, firmly packing the clay. Cover the clay surfaces with the pebbles or glass chips.

2. Arrange the potted plants as desired. Mix the dye with water, if desired, and add the water to the garden until it comes just below the plant stems and foliage.

3. Add the floating plants of your choice. To achieve an effective garden design, don't crowd too many plants into the container. Two to three small potted plants and some floaters make quite an impact. About 70 percent of the water's surface should be covered with plants to retard algae growth.

4. Place the garden in a sunny window facing south or southeast, where it can receive at least four hours of sunlight daily.

5. Aerate the garden by topping it off with more water as water evaporates and by adding a few charcoal chips.

6. As the plants grow, you may use a fertilizer made specifically for water plants. Follow the packaging directions to adjust the amount according the the number of plants and the amount of water in the container.

7. Trim back the plants to keep them well-groomed and shaped.

from the past

Chapter 3

Sometimes older is better. Borrow a few ideas from the Victorians and learn how to say "I love you" with a Flower Message Garden in a basket or embellish your bathroom with a luxuriant Fern Terrarium in a birdcage. Recreate the beloved quilt design called *Moon Over the Mountain* in the Quilted Succulent Garden.

victorian flower message garden

The Victorians assigned special meanings to the flowers and plants they carried or sent to their loved ones. Friendship, congratulations, and many other sentiments were also expressed in floral symbolism. Select among the plants listed to create a garden that describes exactly how you feel. A message garden makes a perfect birthday or hostess gift.

Plants and Their Messages

miniature roses *(Rosa)* **love, passionate and tender**

scented geranium *(Pelargonium* 'Peppermint Tormentosa' *or Pelargonium* 'French Lace'*)* **happiness**

thyme *(Thymus vulgaris)* **daring**

rosemary *(Rosemarinus officialinus)* **remembrance**

gold or tricolor sage *(Salvia officialinus)* **long life**

myrtle *(Myrtus communis)* **my heartfelt love and joy**

ivy *(Hedera)* **wedded love and fidelity**

asparagus fern (*Asparagus Filicinus* **or another variety) sincerity**

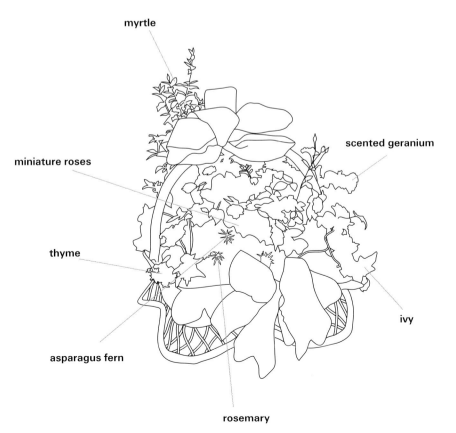

myrtle

miniature roses

scented geranium

thyme

ivy

asparagus fern

rosemary

myrtle *(Myrtus communis)*

miniature roses *(Rosa)*

Tools and Materials

large, strong basket

heavy plastic sheeting, large enough to create two layers in the basket

scissors or screwdriver

potting and planting supplies on page 20

vintage doilies or antimacassars

eyelet lace

floral ribbon

tray or platter big enough to serve as drainage dish

1. Use the plastic sheeting to line the basket and punch a hole in the center to provide drainage.

2. Pour in a 3- to 4-inch (7.6 to 10.2 cm) layer of rich potting soil. Place the plants on top, moving them around until you arrive at a pleasing arrangement. It usually looks best for the larger plants to go in the center or the background.

3. Unpot the plants, reposition them, and fill the spaces between them with soil. Allow enough space at the top to allow watering without overspill.

4. Tuck the doilies over the edges and around the perimeter of the basket, and add bows of eyelet lace and ribbon.

5. Put the garden on top of the drainage dish in an airy location that gets as much sun and warmth as possible. Give it a good watering every three days, then let it dry out but not to the point that the plants fade and wilt. (When the soil shrinks slightly from the sides, this is your sign to water again.)

victorian
fern terrarium

Fern-stuffed parlors and tropical conservatories were all the rage during the time of Queen Victoria. Have you eyed gorgeous but pricey iron-and-glass terrariums, wishing you had the financial resources of a queen? Yearn no more! It's easy to create your own terrarium from a ready-made birdcage by adding cut pieces of sheet glass.

Plants

button fern *(Pellaea rotundifolia)* **in 4-inch (10.2 cm) pots**

staghorn fern *(Playcerium bifurcatum)* **in 4-inch (10.2 cm) pots**

hare's foot fern *(Polypodium aureum mandaiaum)* **in 4-inch (cm) pots**

hare's foot fern
(Polypodium aureum mandaiaum)

button fern *(Pellaea rotundifolia)*

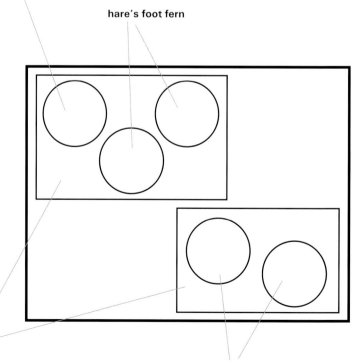

staghorn fern

hare's foot fern

trays

button fern

Tools and Materials

birdcage measuring approximately 18 x 24 x 24 inches (45.7 x 61 x 61 cm), with a removable lid, as shown in the photos

5 pieces of glass cut to fit inside the birdhouse: one for each of the four walls, and one to lay above the garden and beneath the birdhouse lid*

small pieces of polystyrene foam

double-sided masking tape

2 small plastic kitchen trays that can fit on the floor of the birdhouse

dried sheet moss

*A picture framer or local glass supply house can do this for you easily and inexpensively.

1. Slide the pieces of glass inside the four walls of the birdhouse, using bits of the polystyrene foam and double-sided tape to hold them in place if necessary. Place the two trays inside on the floor, as shown in figure 1.

2. Position the potted plants on the trays as shown on page 60, and add enough moss to the floor to come up to the top of the pots and disguise their rims.

3. Lay the fifth sheet of glass over the top of the birdhouse and cover it with the lid.

4. Position the conservatory in a cool, shady spot, and mist and water the plants regularly. Remove the moss and trays when it's time to water or groom the plants.

retro terrariums

Remember when you were a child and you made a terrarium from an old pickle jar, the one that sprouted some fascinating fungi before your mother made you throw it out? This quartet of terrariums is considerably more elegant; the spherical shape of their glass containers evoke 1970s retro style. Limit the number of plants you put in each garden and avoid overcrowding the containers. Less is more.

rainbow vine
(Pellionia pulchra)

Plants

Terrarium #1

strawberry saxifrage *(Saxifraga sarmentosa)*

rainbow vine *(Pellionia pulchra)*

creeping fig *(Ficus pumila)*

club moss *(Selaginella kraussiana)*

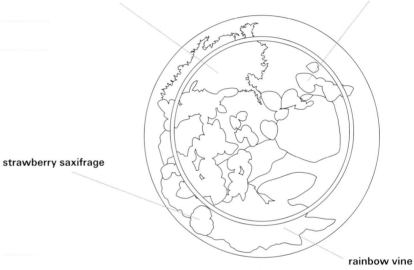

club moss

creeping fig

strawberry saxifrage

rainbow vine

Terrarium #2

strawberry saxifrage *(Saxifraga sarmentosa)*

rainbow vine *(Pellionia pulchra)*

angelwings *(Pilea spruceana 'Norfolk')*

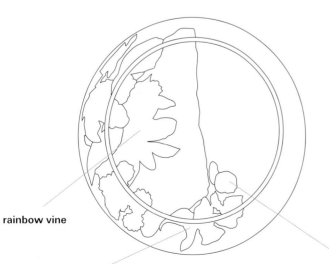

rainbow vine

angelwings

strawberry saxifrage

Terrarium #3

strawberry saxifrage *(Saxifraga sarmentosa)*

creeping fig *(Ficus pumila)*

arrowhead vine *(Syngonium podophyllium)*

club moss *(Selaginella kraussiana)*

strawberry saxifrage *(Saxifraga sarmentosa)*

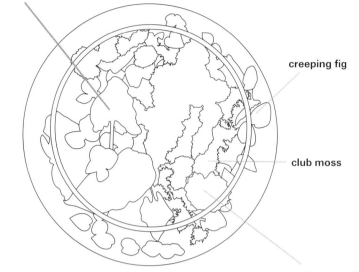

arrowhead vine

creeping fig

club moss

strawberry saxifrage

Terrarium #4

angelwings *(Pilea spruceana 'Norfolk')*

creeping fig *(Ficus pumila)*

baby's tears *(Helxine soleirolii)*

desert privet *(Peperonia magnoliaefolia variegata)*

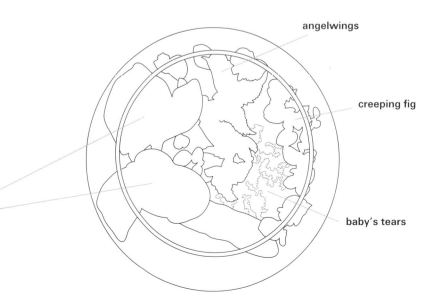

angelwings

creeping fig

baby's tears

desert privet

1. Put a half-inch layer of gravel or other drainage material in the bottom of each container, and add a 2-inch (5 cm) layer of potting soil.

2. Follow the planting diagrams on pages 64 and 65 to add the plants to the terrariums.

3. Keep the gardens in a cool, bright yet indirectly lit location. Since the terrariums are uncovered, you'll need to keep an eye on the soil's moisture content. Water the plants when the soil begins to dry out; if you see the soil begin to change from a dark, wet color to a lighter, drier color, it's time to water. Mist the plants frequently, too.

Tools and Materials

potting and planting supplies on page 20

4 spherical glass containers, 12 to 16 inches (30.5 to 40.6 cm) in circumference

decorative pieces of wood

small rocks

quilted
succulent garden

Planted in the well–known quilt design called *Moon Over the Mountain*, this easy-care garden highlights the spectrum of colors found among succulent plants.

Sedum mexicanum

Sempervivum 'Oddity'

Plants

Sedum mexicanum

Sempervivum 'Oddity'

gravel

Sedum mexicanum

Sempervivum 'Oddity'

Tools and Materials

wooden container, approximately 20 inches
(50.8 cm) square

piece of window screen large enough to
cover drainage hole in container

potting and planting supplies listed on
page 20

black aquarium gravel

drainage saucer

1. This garden design works best if you root your own cut-tings of both types of plants. Refer to step 1 of the Living Succulent Table Wreath on page 123. Allow one month for adequate root development.

2. Place the piece of screen over the container's drainage hole and add a thin layer of potting soil.

3. Plant the cuttings as shown on page 68, and use the aquarium gravel to cover the unplanted area of soil.

4. Place the garden over the drainage saucer in a location that receives day-long, full sun. This will help the plants maintain short, tight growth and the pattern of the garden.

miniature rosemary topiaries

Topiary, the art of training and pruning plants to grow into ornamental shapes, began with the ancient Romans. Rosemary makes fine topiary material, and as long as you keep this Mediterranean native in a sunny location, water sparingly, and provide excellent drainage, it should thrive. You don't even need to feed it unless it's actively growing.

Tools and Materials

2 terra-cotta containers*

potting and planting supplies listed on page 20

hand pruners

dried moss

*The containers shown in the photograph are 4 inches (10.2 cm) in diameter.

Plants

2 small rosemary plant starts *(Rosemarinus officialis)*

common thyme *(Thymus vulgaris)* **(optional)**

1. When selecting the rosemary starts, choose two with growth as strongly vertical as you can find.

2. Pot the starts in the containers.

3. Determine how much of the existing foliage will serve as the "top" of each topiary, and use the pruner to remove all the side shoots below.

4. Use the pruners to shape the tops into roughly spherical shapes. Top pruning also encourages the remaining branches to sprout new growth.

5. Use the dried moss to cover the soil at the base of each topiary. If desired, plant the thyme in the soil underneath the moss, draping it over the edges of the pots.

6. Continue pruning new growth to maintain the tight, thick growth desirable in a topiary.

Topiaries courtesy of The Gardener's Cottage, Biltmore Village, North Carolina

when is a garden not a garden?

Chapter 4

**Expand your idea of what a garden really is.
Make matching Lichen Topiaries. (Did you know
that lichen isn't really a plant?) Build a Fairy
Circle to attract the Little People, or create your
own point of stillness in a Zen Sand Garden.**

fairy circle

Legend has it that late at night when humans have gone to bed, fairies gather in secret meeting places in the forest to dance and be merry. Those places are marked by perfectly round circles or ovals of green grass. Sometimes red and white mushrooms pop up around the perimeter, too. (Red and white are fairies' favorite color, you know.) Here's how to make your own fairy circle to entice the Little People to visit you at home.

reindeer moss *(Cladina or Cladonia)*

Irish moss *(Sagina subulata)*

Plants*

British soldier moss or red caped lichen
(Cladonia cristatella)

galax *(Galax urceolata)*

English ivy *(Hedera)*

Irish moss or Scotch moss *(Sagina subulata or Arenaria verna caespitosa)*

reindeer moss *(Cladina or Cladonia)*

haircap moss *(Polytrichum piliferum)*

puffed shield lichen *(Hypogymnia imshaugii)*

spoon lichen

*Mosses can be purchased from your local nursery, and don't be afraid to use mosses and lichens collected from the ground and fallen branches in your own back yard. (Just be sure to leave some behind to regenerate.)

haircap moss
(Polytrichum piliferum)

galax (Galax urceolata)

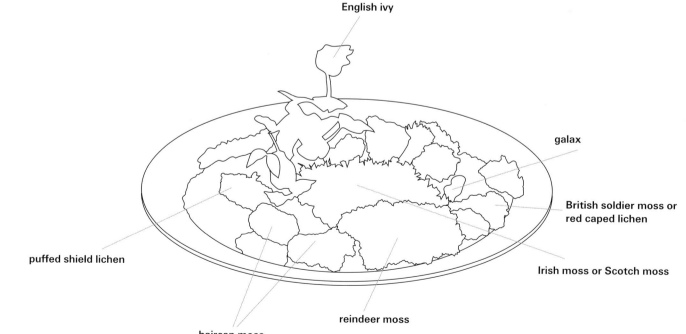

English ivy

galax

British soldier moss or red caped lichen

Irish moss or Scotch moss

reindeer moss

haircap moss

puffed shield lichen

Tools and Materials

shallow, circular container
approximately 14 inches
(35.6 cm) in diameter

potting and planting supplies
listed on page 20

1. Put a shallow layer of drainage material in the container
and add a 1- to 2-inch (2.5 to 5 cm) layer of potting soil.

2. Arrange the mosses, lichens and plants as shown on page
76, gently firming them into the soil. If desired, leave the lichen
on its host wood and add the entire piece to the garden.

3. Mist the garden heavily, and keep the soil moist. Position
the garden in a cool, indirectly lit area that receives some
dappled sunlight.

zen sand garden

Inspired by Far Eastern gardening traditions that are thousands of years old, this exquisitely simple garden uses a single hemlock seedling, careful placement of moss and pebbles, and designs traced in sand to create a miniature oasis of peace and serenity.

1. Make a tiny heap of potting soil in the center of the plate. Wet a small quantity of tissue with water and wad it around the roots of the seedling. Place tree and tissue on the soil.

2. Carefully spread the sand evenly around the plate and around the base of the seedling, covering the soil and some of the tissue. Use dried moss to cover the rest of the tissue. Position the large rock adjacent to the seedling and arrange the pebbles around its base, sinking them slightly into the sand.

3. Use the dinner fork to trace wavy, unbroken lines around the seedling and pebbles. Add more lines, creating a pattern that spreads outward to the edges of the plate, somewhat like the ripples created by throwing a rock in a pond.

4. Put the garden in a cool, indirectly lit location and every few days, pour a tiny amount of water at the base of the seedling.

Tools and Materials

large dinner plate with gold finish*

small quantity of potting soil

bath or facial tissue

sand, about 3 to 4 cups (0.75 kg)

dried moss

8 to 10 small, smooth pebbles

1 fist-size rock

dinner fork

*If you have a plate of a different color, spray-paint it with metallic gold paint.

Plants

evergreen tree seedling, such as a longleaf pine (*Pinus palustris*), or an eastern hemlock (*Tsuga canadensis*)

eastern hemlock (*Tsuga canadensis*)

Japanese forest grass
(*Hakonechloa macra* 'Aureola')

'Little Bunny' miniature fountain grass
(*Pennisetum alopecuroides* 'Little Bunny')

Madagascar dragon tree
(*Draceaena marginata*)

sensory grass garden

Color, fragrance, *and* sound! This gorgeous garden is designed to take advantage of the amazing variety of colors, textures, and even smells found among members of the grass family. Golden, bamboolike Japanese forest grass, black and silver mondo grasses, and white-flowering fountain grass provide visual pleasure. Lightly crush a frond of sweet flag and inhale its fragrance. If you place this garden in a breezy spot, you can enjoy the sound of the wind rustling through the fronds.

yellow sweet flag
(*Acorus gramineus* 'Ogon')

black mondo grass
(*Ophiopogon planiscapus* 'Arabicus')

Plants

Japanese forest grass *(Hakonechloa macra* **'Aureola'***)*

'Little Bunny' miniature fountain grass *(Pennisetum alopecuroides* **'Little Bunny'***)*

black mondo grass *(Ophiopogon planiscapus* **'Arabicus'***)*

silver mondo grass *(Ophiopogon* **'Silver Mist'***)*

Madagascar dragontree *(Draceaena marginata)*

yellow sweet flag *(Acorus gramineus* **'Ogon'***)*

'Little Bunny' miniature fountain grass

Madagascar dragon tree

yellow sweet flag

black mondo grass

Japanese forest grass

silver mondo grass

Tools and Materials

basket, 12 to 24 inches (30.5 to 61 cm) in diameter and 6 to 12 inches (15.2 to 30.5 cm) high

waterproof plastic liner sized to fit the basket

potting and planting supplies listed on page 20

fresh or dried moss

large rock, small piece of wood, or driftwood in an interesting shapea

1. Place the liner in the basket. You may choose to arrange the individually potted grasses in the basket, or plant them together in the container.

2. Cover the bases of the grasses and any exposed soil with moss, and add the decorative stone or wood accent.

3. Place the garden in a sunny location where it can receive at least two to three hours of sunlight daily. Keep the soil moist.

4. Groom the plants by trimming them back to pleasing heights. Grasses are tough, so don't be afraid to be creative with your scissors!

Plants courtesy of Reems Creek Nursery, Weaverville, North Carolina

scented geranium boudoir garden

It's wonderful to wake up to a fragrant garden on a nearby table. This unusual garden incorporates a wide variety of geraniums with leaves of differing textures and amazing scents, including apple, nutmeg, and even coconut! Cuttings are planted in handmade, cylindrical porcelain containers and placed on top of an old silver tray. Add some wired ribbon or mesh in muted colors to the tray handles if you like.

Plants*

Pelargonium 'Peppermint Tormentosa'

Pelargonium 'Spiced Apple'

Pelargonium 'French Lace'

Pelargonium 'Lemon Crispum'

Pelargonium 'Mabel Gray'

Pelargonium 'Cody's Nutmeg'

Pelargonium 'Lady Mary'

Pelargonium 'Coconut'

Pelargonium 'Pheasant's Foot'

*If your local nursery doesn't stock all the varieties you want, you can order them by mail from specialty nurseries.

Pelargonium 'Peppermint Tormentosa'

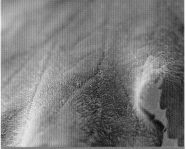

Pelargonium 'Lemon Crispum'

Pelargonium 'Spiced Apple'

Tools and Materials

8 to 10 small, cylindrical ceramic or porcelain containers*

potting and planting supplies listed on page 20

dried moss

metal tray

wired ribbon (optional)

*Using containers of different heights creates an attractive effect. The tallest container shown in the photograph is 6 inches (15.2 cm) and the shortest, 4 inches (10.2 cm).

1. Use rich potting soil to plant cuttings of each geranium, one per container, and cover the soil with a little dried moss.

2. If the tray has handles, embellish them with the wired ribbon if desired. Set the tray in a location that receives lots of sun and fresh air, and arrange the containers of cuttings on the tray. Use more dried moss to fill in the spaces between the containers.

lichen topiaries

These paired topiaries make a stunning sculptural accent in an entrance hall when placed on a low table or flanking a couch. They're made of surprisingly simple materials including grey lichen, which you can gather from fallen tree limbs or purchase at craft stores. Technically, lichen isn't a plant. It's what results when a fungus of the *Ascomycetes* class combines with algae. But however you look at it, this unusual material helps provide a witty and contemporary interpretation of the topiary arts.

gray lichen *(Ascomycetes)*

Plants

gray lichen *(Ascomycetes)*

rooted needlepoint ivy
(Hedera helix)

milk cactus
(Euphorbia tirucalli)

Tools and Materials

4 polystyrene foam balls, 8 to 10 inches (20.3 to 25.4 cm) in diameter

long knife with a thin blade

strong craft glue

2 slim, straight tree branches, each about 1/2 inch (1.3 cm) in diameter and 3 feet (0.9 m) long*

paper towels or rags

2 plastic plant pots, 6-inch (15.2 cm)

2 ceramic planters (the ones shown in the photograph are about 18 inches [45.7 cm] tall)

5-pound (2.27 kg) bag of plaster**

bucket

spoon or other mixing tool

bucket or other container

spool of thin-gauge galvanized wire or florist's greening pins, also called U pins

plant mister filled with water

wire cutters

*The designer used the remains of two deceased topiary trees and wired wadded-up plastic grocery bags into ball shapes around the bare twigs before applying the lichen. But polystyrene foam balls make a fine alternative to dead topiaries!

**Available at craft stores

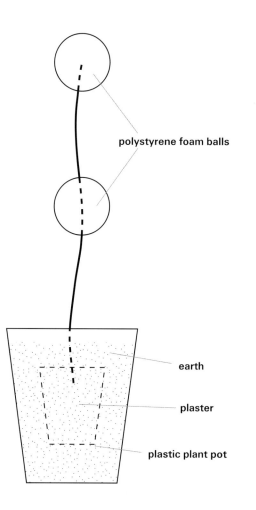

polystyrene foam balls

earth

plaster

plastic plant pot

1. Use the knife to mark the exact centerpoint of each foam ball. Working with the first two balls, carve a small hole through the middle, making sure the holes are smaller than the diameter of the tree branches. Carve holes of similar diameter in the remaining two balls, but don't carve all the way through (these two balls will top the topiaries).

2. Refer to the diagram above. Squirt or pour a generous amount of the craft glue into the holes of the first two balls, and immediately insert a branch through each one, positioning the sphere a little above the midpoint of the branch. Wipe off any glue remaining on the branch. Let dry.

3. Add glue to the holes in the remaining two balls, then affix a ball atop each branch. Let dry.

4. Mix enough plaster to fill both 6-inch (15.2 cm) pots. Insert the branches into the plaster, one per pot, bracing them so they stand up straight. Let the plaster dry about an hour until it's completely hardened.

5. The most critical part of lichen craft is to wet the material and work with it while it's still pliable. Soak the lichen in the bucket filled with water until it's saturated and flexible but not starting to disintegrate.

6. Use the wire or U pins to secure the wet lichen to the foam balls, applying a generous amount of lichen. (The wire disappears into the lichen as you tighten it.) Keep misting the lichen with water if necessary to maintain its pliability. When finished, cut the wire and hide the end in the lichen.

7. Position the potted branches inside the ceramic containers, as shown on the previous page. Add the soil, bringing it 1 or 2 inches (2.5 to 5 cm) beneath the rim of the containers. Tamp and wet the soil as you fill the containers.

8. Cover the soil with the sheet moss, then plant sprigs of rooted ivy and milk cactus as desired under the moss.

9. The lichen becomes brittle as it dries, so position the topiaries away from direct sun. Mist the lichen periodically with water and it will "live" for years.

bottle garden

"How did you do that?" You'll hear that a lot from visitors who see this charming bottle garden. Kids are particularly fascinated by things in miniature, and this garden makes a great family project.

Plants

mosses*

gray lichen *(Ascomycetes)**

***Plants gathered from your backyard will work beautifully.**

Tools and Materials

potting and planting supplies on page 20, including pulverized charcoal

glass bottle with a neck large enough to accommodate chopsticks*

iced tea spoon (optional)

chopsticks or surgical tweezers**

*Specialty vinegar or olive oil bottles may be suitable.

**Surgical tweezers are available at medical supply stores.

1. Using the iced tea spoon if necessary, add charcoal to the bottle. Shake the bottle gently to distribute it in an even layer on the bottom.

2. Add a layer of soil to the bottle.

3. Using the chopsticks or tweezers, add bits of moss to the bottle, gently tamping them down. Pour in a little water to moisten the garden, and mist it heavily. Keep the garden moist and in an indirectly lit location, especially while the moss takes root.

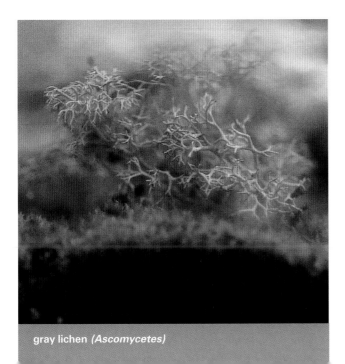

gray lichen *(Ascomycetes)*

from
faraway places

Chapter 5

These designs are inspired by cultures that were already creating world-famous gardens and landscapes many thousands of years ago. Here's how to build your own Hanging Gardens of Babylon and assemble a beautiful Bagua Garden based on an ancient Chinese design.

hanging gardens of babylon

Almost 4,000 years ago, King Hammurabi's terraced gardens on the banks of the Euphrates were one of the seven wonders of the world. Stack containers of diminishing sizes on each other, and you've created your own mini-ziggurat, much like the stepped pyramids of ancient times. You'll plant this garden with dramatically colored plants to heighten its exotic look. *Impatiens cristata* is particularly striking with its tiny leaves, red stems, and flowers shaped like wild touch-me-nots, but you may use any variety of impatiens you like.

wandering jew *(Tradescantia)*

golden oregano *(Origanum vulgare* 'Aureum'*)*

Impatiens cristata

Plants

wandering jew *(Tradescantia)*

tricolor sedum (*Sedum spurium* 'Tricolor')

Impatiens cristata

golden oregano (*Origanum vulgare* 'Aureum')

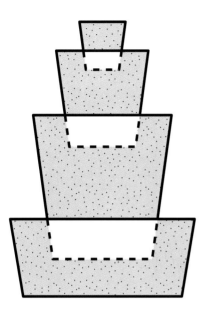

Tools and Materials

4 terra-cotta pots in diminishing diameters of 16, 12, 8, and 4 inches (40.6, 30.5, 20.3, and 10.2 cm)*

drainage saucer sized to fit the largest pot

potting and planting supplies listed on page 20

*The 16-inch (40.6 cm) pot is actually a lower-profile container called an azalea pot.

1. Because of the size of this garden, it's easiest to construct it where it will live full-time. These plants love sun, so find a sunny tabletop and put the drainage saucer in position.

2. Refer to the figure at left. Fill the largest pot half-full of potting soil, and line the outer edges of the pot with wandering jew, tricolor sedum, and impatiens. Remember, odd numbers of plants look better!

3. Fit the next-largest pot inside the first, centering it over the bare soil in the middle of the largest pot. Add soil to cover plant roots and to anchor the second pot on top of the first. Tamp the soil to keep the pot from wiggling but not so much as to compress and compact the soil.

4. Fill the second pot half-full of soil and plant golden oregano around its outer perimeter. Place the third pot in the middle, adding additional soil and tamping it as before.

5. Fill the third pot half-full of soil, and plant wandering jew around the perimeter. Add soil and tamp it down.

6. Top the garden with the fourth pot, securing it with earth. Plant it with impatiens. Since the pots are half-full of soil, remember that they'll dry out fairly quickly and will need frequent watering. They're so beautiful, it's worth it!

spirit and matter garden

The design for this simple yet stunning garden is taken from the famous Chalice Well of Glastonbury, England, one of the oldest sacred sites in the world. Legend says that the Holy Grail lies hidden in the well. Like the cover of the well itself, this garden incorporates a *Vesica Piscis*, an oval formed by two interlinking circles, representing the process of creation and the intermingling of spirit and matter.

Plants

hen and chickens *(Sempervivum tectorum)*, **approximately 200**

hen and chickens *(Sempervivum tectorum)*

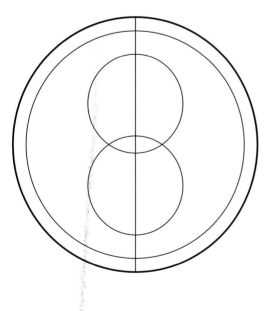

Tools and Materials

circular container 14 inches (35.6 cm) in diameter and 2 to 3 inches (5 to 7.6 cm) deep

black cactus sand*

potting and planting supplies listed on page 20

2 plastic nursery pots: one 6 inches (15.2 cm) in diameter and one 10 inches (25.4 cm) in diameter

*Available at home improvement stores

dle of the circle. Finally, use the smaller pot to press two smaller, interlinking circles, as shown in the figure on the preceding page. Your purpose is to create shallow valleys in the sand in which you can plant the succulents.

3. Position the plants in the lines drawn in the sand, and use more sand to fill in the valleys around the base of the plants to create a smooth surface.

4. Use a mister bottle filled with water to wash any sand from the tops of the rosettes. Spray around and underneath the rosettes to further anchor them.

5. Hen and chickens like hot, dry locations, but the garden should be located in a spot that receives as much medium-intensity light as possible with moderate temperatures. You can thus prolong the garden's life and avoid overheating the black sand in the shallow container, which would "cook" the plants.

6. Water sparingly and use a handheld mister or mister nozzle on a hose to clean off any sand that drifts over the plants. Withhold fertilizer during the winter.

1. Put a layer of drainage material and a layer of potting soil in the container. Top with a layer of the black cactus sand, reserving some sand for later use.

2. Refer to the diagram on page 98. Centering the largest nursery pot over the container, press a circle on the surface of the sand. Use a trowel to draw a straight line through the mid-

orchid fantasy garden

Have you fantasized about growing orchids indoors but thought you had to have a full-blown greenhouse and other exotic paraphernalia to do so? Not so. *Phaeleonopsis* are among the easiest orchids to grow indoors. A group of these tropical beauties on your table will have a stunning impact.

Plants

3 to 4 striped *Phaeleonopsis* *Dendrobium* **orchids**

Tools and Materials

3 rectangular wooden or pottery containers of varying heights

newspaper

silver spray paint

clear spray-on acrylic sealer in mat finish (optional)

3 plastic liners, sized to fit inside the containers

potting and planting supplies listed on page 20

dried moss

orchid food

1. Place the containers on newspaper and spray-paint them. After they've dried, finish with a coat of the sealer on the outside to dull down the finish if desired. Let dry.

2. After putting layers of drainage material and compost in the plastic liners, position the orchids inside. Fill in spaces with compost, and add a top dressing of the dried moss. The moss helps retain moisture and means less watering, but push the moss aside when you water so as to avoid wetting the moss, thereby keeping the crowns of the plants dry. Pour off any water that pools in the bottom of the container; orchids demand good drainage.

3. Fertilize the gardens weekly, using a very diluted solution of orchid food. An important tip: When flowering has finished, don't cut off the bloom spike! It will flower again when a new spike grows from the base of the plant; orchids can grow multiple spikes that flower simultaneously. You can encourage the formation of new spikes by putting the gardens in a location that has a 55°F (13°C) nighttime temperature during the fall season.

curly bamboo garden

A beloved symbol of long life and luck to the Chinese, bamboo has become increasingly popular in the West. Despite its name, curly bamboo is actually a member of the lily family, although its segmented canes resemble bamboo. A very tough and resilient plant, curly bamboo doesn't form a spiral pattern naturally. Growers manipulate its exposure to light to create the pattern and it can take a year or more to make a single curl. Children will enjoy creating this simple garden and checking the progress of its root formation from time to time.

Plants

3 canes of curly bamboo, lucky bamboo, or ribbon plant *(Dracaena sanderiana)*, each about 8 to 10 inches (20.3 to 25.4 cm) long*

*Each section should contain 4 or 5 joints (the raised areas that ring the cane at periodic intervals). Leaves will sprout from the top and joints.

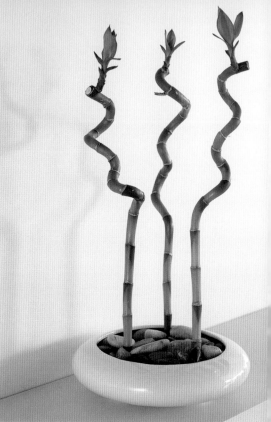

Tools and Materials

low ceramic container, the kind used for forcing bulbs*

smooth pebbles

*If desired, use a taller container filled with more water to
encourage more abundant root growth.

1. Fill the container with the pebbles, leaving enough room for the bamboo canes.

2. Insert the canes into the pebble-filled container, spacing them equally. Add 1 to 3 inches (2.5 to 7.6 cm) of water, making sure one or more joints are below the waterline. Add more pebbles to help stabilize the cuttings and keep them upright.

3. The garden will thrive for years in very low to bright, indirect light. Keep the water topped up at the same level and change it every two to three weeks. To encourage leaves to grow, add a drop of liquid plant food to the water periodically. The longer the leaves are, the more good fortune they're said to bring!

bagua garden

This lovely garden is based on the design of the bagua, the nine-sector grid used in the ancient Chinese art of Feng Shui to harmonize and balance the energies within a home. Each sector of the bagua is associated with specific colors, and each sector influences an important aspect of our lives. You'll use plants and metal pipe or gravel to create your own Bagua Garden. Clockwise from the top, the nine sectors of the bagua are: Fame, Relationship, Children and Creativity, Travel and Helpful People, Life's Path, Knowledge, Health and Family, Wealth, and the Center.

Plants*

hen and chicks *(Sempervivum tectorum* 'Red Beauty'*)*

tricolor sedum *(Sedum spurium* 'Tricolor'*), Sedum linearis, and/or Kalanchoe pumila*

dunce caps *(Orostachys furusei)*

feather cactus *(Mammillaria plumosa)*

Sedum mexicanum

Aeonium arboreum 'Zwartkop'

sedum acre *(Sedum album)*

bugleweed *(Ajuga valfredda* 'Chocolate Chip'*)*

Sedum 'Ogon'

*Starting at the center top of the garden shown in the photograph, the plants are arranged in a clockwise direction.

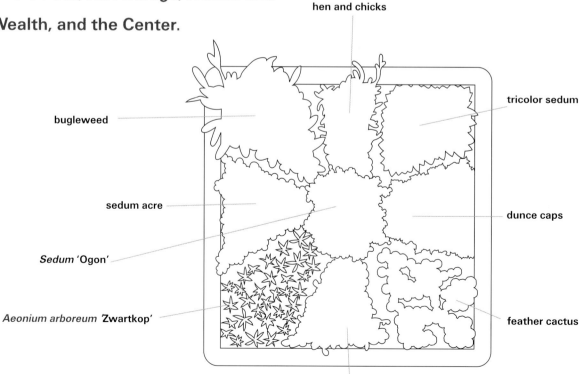

hen and chicks

bugleweed

tricolor sedum

sedum acre

dunce caps

Sedum 'Ogon'

Aeonium arboreum 'Zwartkop'

feather cactus

Sedum mexicanum

hen and chicks (*Sempervivum tectorum* 'Red Beauty')

tricolor sedum (*Sedum spurium* 'Tricolor')

feather cactus (*Mammillaria plumosa*)

Sedum mexicanum

sedum acre (*Sedum album*)

Sedum 'Ogon'

bugleweed (*Ajuga valfredda* 'Chocolate Chip')

dunce caps (*Orostachys furusei*)

Tools and Materials

large, square ceramic container*

power drill (optional)

drainage tray large enough to position under the container

plastic liner with drainage hole, sized to fit the container (optional)

potting and planting supplies listed on page 20

8 short sections of metal pipe** or colored aquarium gravel

metal ruler

assorted decorative objects of your choice: shells for the Life's Path sector; candles for the Fame sector; pebbles or crystals for Knowledge, Relationship, and the Center; and metal objects for Children and Creativity and Helpful People and Travel

*The container shown in the photograph is 16 inches (40.6 cm) square and about 5 inches (12.7 cm) high

**Adapt the length of the pipes to fit the container of your choice.

1. Drainage is extremely important in maintaining the health of the Bagua Garden. If your container doesn't have a drainage hole, drill one in the bottom or have it done at your local home improvement center. Alternatively, use a plastic liner (with drainage hole) to line the container and be diligent about pouring off excess water.

2. Working at least a month before you wish to plant the Bagua Garden, prepare several dozen cuttings of each plant by following the technique described in step 1 of the Living Succulent Table Wreath (page 123).

3. Put a 1-inch (2.5 cm) layer of gravel in the bottom of the container and cover it with a 2-inch (5 cm) layer of potting soil.

4. Using the metal ruler, mark out the nine sectors of the bagua as shown in the photo at left. Position the pipes along the marks or carefully sprinkle the colored gravel along the lines.

5. Using a dibber or other pointed tool, plant the rooted cuttings in the order shown on page 106. If you're using colored gravel, sprinkle more gravel between the sectors of the bagua and around the center if necessary to highlight the design.

6. If desired, add decorative or symbolic objects to selected areas of the bagua.

7. Position the garden on top of the drainage tray in a location where it will receive a few hours of morning sun. Water sparingly. During the summer only, feed it with a dilute solution of liquid houseplant food. Withhold food during the winter, and mist it frequently to counter the effects of dry indoor air.

gardens seasonal & unseasonal

Chapter 6

Spring, winter, summer, and fall. Whether you enjoy the midwinter blooms of a Daffodil Dish Garden or you craft a Living Succulent Table Wreath to use as holiday decoration, you'll learn how to propagate all sorts of plants while creating beautiful gardens. Love the feel of grass under your feet? Make your own tickle-your-toes mini-meadow with the Living Tabletop Garden.

welcome springtime daffodil dish gardens

The cheerful face of the daffodil, a member of the family *Narcissus*, may be our best-known floral harbinger of spring. But why wait for blooms when you can force bulbs to flower indoors long before spring? Here's how.

Plants

daffodil bulbs in a size as large as you can afford, 1 to 3 bulbs per pot

*In general, the larger the bulb is, the larger the flower.

Tools and Materials

painted ceramic bowls, twice as deep as the height of a bulb

potting and planting supplies listed on page 20

1. When you force daffodils or any other bulb, you trick them into blooming prematurely by putting them in a dark place with a temperature that remains between 33 and 45°F (0.5 and 7.1°C) for a set amount of time, in effect creating an artificial winter. Once removed from the cold and dark, the bulbs think it's spring and time to bloom!

2. When planting the daffodils in the bowls, place the largest bulb at the center bottom of a bowl and flank it with smaller bulbs. Follow the forcing instructions on page 15. If you wish to use bulbs other than daffodils in your tabletop garden, refer to the Cooling Periods chart on page 15 for their particular cooling times. To combine different bulbs, plant them in smaller containers, then repot them after they begin to flower.

3. After the gardens start to flower, place them on a tabletop in a cool, indirectly lit location. Allow the surface of the soil to dry out slightly between waterings.

living tabletop garden

This is tabletop gardening at its most literal! If you can operate a jigsaw or you have a helpful friend who's knowledgeable in woodworking, it's easy to install ready-made planters in a wooden coffee table from the flea market. Fill the planters with wheat grass and you can enjoy the sensation of grass tickling your bare feet—in the comfort of your living room. Why wait for summer?

Plants

packets of seed or flats of wheatgrass

*Check with your local nursery for a variety appropriate for your region.**

Tools and Materials

rectangular plastic planters or window boxes constructed with a lip that runs around the rim*

tape measure

ruler or straightedge

pencil

coffee table or other low wooden table of your choice**

jigsaw

sandpaper

tack cloth

paintbrush

latex acrylic paint in color desired for the table

alcohol or other solvent

clean rags

newspaper

spray paint to match or coordinate with the table's color (optional)

potting and planting supplies listed on page 20

*After you determine how many planters you'd like to install in your table, buy at least double that amount. This allows you to stagger planting times of the grass and change out the planters as needed. The planters are sold at home improvement centers.

**Use a table with a wooden top thick enough to support the weight of at least two planters filled with dirt and grass.

1. If you wish to grow your own wheatgrass, start at step 5 to prepare the planters, then add soil and seeds. Provide lots of sun and moisture and allow 4 to 8 days for the seeds to sprout. Seed the remaining planters two to three weeks later; you can use these to replace the first two, when the grass starts to die back.

2. Measure the dimensions of a planter at a point immediately under its projecting lip. Transfer those dimensions to the coffee table, drawing outlines where you wish to install the planters in the table. Two planters, placed end to end in a standard-size coffee table, creates a nice effect.

3. Use the jigsaw to cut out the holes you outlined.

4. Sand the table, wipe it clean with the tack cloth, and paint it as desired. Let dry.

5. Use the alcohol and rags to clean the planters, then set them on newspaper and paint them. Let dry.

6. Fill the planters with potting soil and seed, or top them with wheatgrass starts from a nursery.

7. When the grass has achieved the desired lushness, lower the planters into the holes in the table. Their rims will keep them suspended. Ideally, the table should be located in an area with lots of sunlight and cooler temperatures. Lower light intensity creates elongated, floppy grass. The brighter the location, the longer the grass will last. Change out the planters as needed.

tabletop cutting garden

This project is a wonderful way to create a tabletop garden from stem or tip cuttings of plants you already have. Once their roots have developed, you can plant them in pots if you wish. This garden incorporates plants that root so readily they can be started in plain tap water. Use a ceramic container, rather than a clear glass bowl, to promote root growth. For a pretty effect, you can also use smaller containers in multiples.

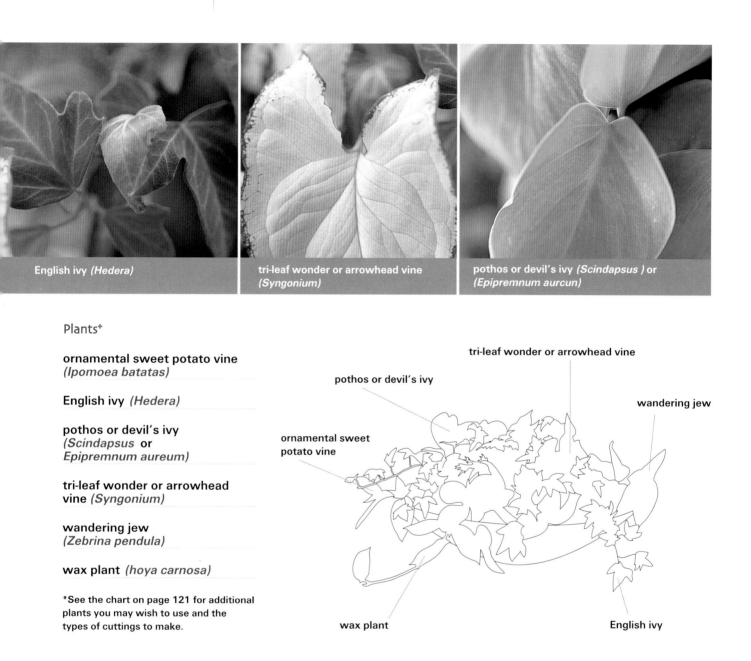

English ivy *(Hedera)*

tri-leaf wonder or arrowhead vine *(Syngonium)*

pothos or devil's ivy *(Scindapsus)* or *(Epipremnum aurcun)*

Plants*

ornamental sweet potato vine
(Ipomoea batatas)

English ivy *(Hedera)*

pothos or devil's ivy
(Scindapsus or Epipremnum aureum)

tri-leaf wonder or arrowhead vine *(Syngonium)*

wandering jew
(Zebrina pendula)

wax plant *(hoya carnosa)*

*See the chart on page 121 for additional plants you may wish to use and the types of cuttings to make.

pothos or devil's ivy

tri-leaf wonder or arrowhead vine

ornamental sweet potato vine

wandering jew

wax plant

English ivy

Tools and Materials

sharp knife or pruning shears

waterproof ceramic container, or a basket with a waterproof liner or bowl inside

clean pebbles, tumbled glass chips, or colored gravel

aquarium grade charcoal*

*Sold in pet stores

1. Layer the pebbles in the container deep enough to hold the cuttings while allowing the cuttings' tips or foliage to emerge above the container rim.

2. Prepare leaf cuttings by referring to the chart on the next page and cutting tips or non-flowering sections of stem, 4 to 6 inches (10.2 to 15.2 cm) long. Each section should have two nodes or sets of leaves. Morning is the best time to take cuttings, because the stems are full of moisture. Use a sharp knife or pruning shears to sever the cutting at a 45° angle just above an outward-facing leaf node. Refer again to the chart on this page for the types of cuttings you can take from different plants.

3. Mix the pebbles and charcoal at a proportion of one part pebbles to 10 parts charcoal, and put a layer in the bottom of the container. Gently place the cuttings in the container, securing them in the pebble-and-charcoal mixture without crushing them. Fill the container with tap water to a point just below the top of the container.

4. Position the garden in a bright, indirectly lit location. Keep the water clean by adding charcoal chips and topping off with more water as needed, which will keep the water aerated. Many cuttings can stay in the same water for up to a month with a few top-ups. Some actually root better if they're grouped together and the water isn't changed, because the cuttings produce a natural rooting hormone, which would be discarded with a change of water.

5. Feed the garden with a very dilute solution of plant food mixed to one quarter the strength recommended for plants growing in soil. If roots are forming rapidly, feed weekly. Otherwise, fertilize only after roots begin to appear.

6. Once roots have formed, transplant the cuttings to earth-filled pots if desired. This will vary from plant to plant. Rooting often takes longer in the lower-light winter months. You may add more new cuttings to replenish your garden and keep it looking fresh and interesting for several months. Some cuttings, such as pothos, wax plant, or arrowhead vine last for years!

easy rooting plants & cutting guide

NAME OF PLANT	TYPE(S) OF CUTTINGS
aluminum plant (Pilea cadierea)	tip
arrowhead vine (Syngonium)	stem
begonia	tip and stem
Chinese evergreen (Aglaeonema)	tip
coleus	tip
Cordyline terminalis	tip
devil's ivy or pothos (Pothos aureus)	tip and stem
dumb cane (Dieffenbachia)	tip
geranium (Pelargonium)	tip
impatiens	tip
ivy (Hedera)	stem
jade plant (Crassula)	tip
philodendron	tip and stem
Swedish ivy (Plectranthus)	tip and stem
ti plant (Dracaena)	stem and tip
wandering jew (Zebrina pendula)	stem and tip
wax plant or wax flower (Hoya carnosa)	tip

living succulent table wreath

This living wreath makes a stunning addition to a table set for the holidays or it can grace your table year-round. Insert candles if you want to heighten its romantic effect. You'll also learn the best way to root and culture succulent plants.

Plants

blue echeveria *(Echeveria glauca)*

silver crown *(Cotyledon undulata)*

mistletoe cactus *(Rhipsalis cassutha)*

chain cactus *(Rhipsalis paradoxa)*

zipper cactus or rat tail cactus *(Crassula lycopodiodes)*

blue sedum *(Sedum mexicanum)*

variegated jade plant *(Portulacaria afra* 'Variegata'*)*

zipper cactus or rat tail cactus *(Crassula lycopodiodes)*

Tools and Materials

rectangle of burlap, about 12 inches (30.5 cm) wide by 4 feet (1.2 m) long

thin-gauge wire

potting and planting supplies on page 20

rooting hormone*

scissors

dibber, or other pointed tool suitable for making holes to plant cuttings

tub or other container big enough to hold the wreath

dried moss

U pins, also called florist's greening pins

liquid houseplant food

pillar candles (optional)

*Make sure the rooting hormone contains the ingredient IBA (indole butyric acid).

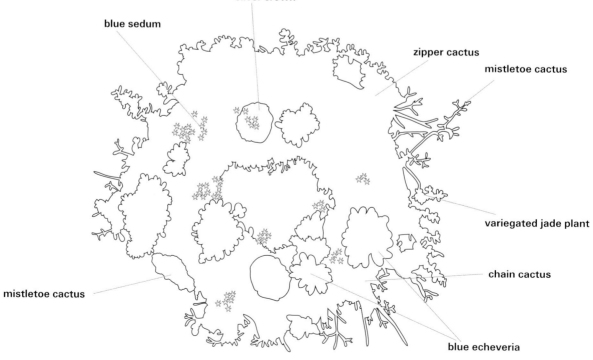

1. Working at least a month prior to the time you'd like to assemble your wreath, make dozens of rooted cuttings of the plants. After they've been snipped from the mother plant, succulents take a few days to several weeks for a callous to form over the "wound." Roots then grow from that spot or other places on the stem when inserted into soil. Unlike woody plants, ivy, or other plants that root in water, it is not helpful for succulent cuttings to stay wet; rot may occur.

2. Prepare the wreath form by wrapping the long edges of the burlap together and using the wire to "sew" them together, creating a tube. Fill the tube with potting soil, then bend it to form a circle and wire the ends together.

3. Apply rooting hormone to the "planting" ends of the cuttings. Using the scissors if necessary, snip or poke holes in the burlap and insert the rooted cuttings into the soil inside the burlap form.

4. Position the wreath so it receives bright, indirect light. Water it frequently by soaking it in a tub of water, then setting it in a sink or another place to drip dry. Once the plantings are established, the wreath can be watered sparingly and kept fairly dry.

5. A few weeks after planting, moisten the dried moss with enough water to make it very pliable. Using the U pins, fasten moss to the underside of the wreath. On the front side of the wreath, tuck small pieces of moss into any spaces between plants to cover the burlap. It's also almost inevitable that some plants will have expired, so add new rooted cuttings where desired.

6. During the summer only, feed the wreath with a dilute solution of liquid houseplant food and, if possible, place it outdoors for a few hours of morning sun. (Don't leave it to roast outside in the afternoon.) In winter, don't feed the wreath, mist it frequently to counter dry indoor air and keep it away from direct drafts of hot air from a furnace or wood stove.

7. For a festive effect, sink pillar candles into the table wreath. Remember, never leave burning candles unattended.

Acknowledgments

This beautiful book is the product of the labors of many talented people, including art director Tom Metcalf, photographer Steve Mann, and all the wonderful designers whose work is featured in these pages.

Thank you to everyone who generously allowed us to use their homes and businesses as photo locations, including Sandi and Dave Bowman, Richard Fort, Steven Frost, and Steve Parker of The Screen Door in Asheville. Thanks also to the staff at Reems Creek Valley Nursery in Weaverville, North Carolina for their friendly and expert advice and to The Gardener's Cottage in Biltmore Village, North Carolina for their assistance.

In closing, I'd like to express my gratitude to my delightful friend and gardener extraordinaire Christopher Mello. This book wouldn't have happened without his amazing knowledge of things botanical, marvellous design sensibility, and nimble assistance. Thank you, Christopher.

Designers and Contributors

Susan Kinney is a designer specializing in eclectic interiors, glass and clay jewelry, fabric and rug design, and computer generated artwork. She has a B.A. in Art History, a B.F.A. in Sculpture/Ceramics, and more than 30 years' experience in interior and landscape design, raku pottery, and wearable art. Her work is inspired in part by the cultures of Hawaii and Japan, where she lived for more than 20 years. <susan@suezen.com>

Corinne Kurzmann enjoys an eclectic life as the mother of 10 children and owner of Diggin Art, a retail and landscaping business in Asheville, North Carolina. A gardener all her life, Corinne also creates decorative objects and jewelry from vintage materials. Her work has been featured in more than a dozen Lark books.

Christopher D. Mello is a horticulturist by trade (but prefers to call himself a gardener), and he gained much of his experience on the grounds of the historic Biltmore Estate in his hometown of Asheville, North Carolina. He is also an accomplished metal sculptor, floral designer, and ceramist. His garden is open during daylight hours. 6 Riverside Drive, Asheville, NC, 28801, (828) 255-8648

Marla Murphy keeps busy with her own gardening and weeding, having retired from her previous occupation running an herb farm in North Carolina. Also a professional photographer, her interest grew in design and graphics during her years with an ad agency in Denver, where she learned to get along with utter lunatics in the ad business.

Ben Waters currently devotes his free time to hybridizing day lilies. A self-taught hobby gardener all his life, he is retired from a 25-year career in the nursery business and divides his time between Asheville, North Carolina and Greenville, South Carolina.

Jane Wilson spent many years as a studio designer, after studying art history and design at East Tennessee University and technical drawing and drafting at Eastern Kentucky University. She is gifted in gardening and many other media, including fiber arts. P.O. Box 992, Black Mountain, North Carolina, 28711.

Index